IMAGED WORDS
&
WORDED IMAGES

EDITED AND WITH AN INTRODUCTION
BY RICHARD KOSTELANETZ

OUTERBRIDGE & DIENSTFREY
DISTRIBUTED BY E. P. DUTTON & COMPANY

For S. G. B., whose affectionate sympathy
Turned this dream, and much else, into realities.

Other Books by Richard Kostelanetz

As Author:
Metamorphosis in the Arts
Master Minds
The Theatre of Mixed Means

As Co-Author and Editor:
The New American Arts

As Editor:
Social Speculations
John Cage
Moholy-Nagy
Possibilities of Poetry
Beyond Left and Right
The Young American Writers
Twelve from the Sixties
On Contemporary Literature

Library of Congress number 76—106613
First published in the United States of America in 1970
Copyright © 1970 by Richard Kostelanetz
All rights reserved including the right of reproduction
in whole or in part in any form.
Manufactured in the United States of America
First Printing

Outerbridge & Dienstfrey
200 West 72nd Street
New York, 10023

INTRODUCTION

Conductors of an enormous orchestra, (modern poets) will have at their disposal the whole world, its sounds and appearances, the thought and the human languages, song, dance, all the arts and all the artifices to compose the book seen and understood by the future.

—Guillaume Apollinaire, Chroniques d'Art

The artist sees and feels not only shapes but words as well. We see words everywhere in modern life; we're bombarded by them. But physically words are also shapes. You don't want banal boring words any more than you want banal boring shapes or a banal boring life.

—Stuart Davis, as quoted by Katherine Kuh, The Artist's Voice (1960).

A new art necessarily demands a new name, and the art of incorporating word within image has recently inspired a spate of new names "calligrams," "concrete poetry," "ideograms," "pattern poems," "concretism." They all are intended to identify artifacts that are neither word nor image alone but somewhere or something between. Since each of the terms in actual usage defines a particular strain of word-image art, there is a need for a more general yet discriminating term. My choice is "word-imagery," which encompasses the two major genres of the form—imaged words and worded images. The distinction depends upon whether word or image is the base. In imaged words, a significant word or phrase is endowed with a visual form, so that language is enhanced through *pictorial* means. In worded images, in contrast, language fills an image, embellishing the shape through linguistic means so that a picture of, say, an ice-cream cone filled with words offers an experience considerably different from that of a cone without words. The difference is the difference between visually laying out a poetic nugget (imaged words) and making pictures with words and letters.

Though our awareness of word-imagery as a distinct art is rather recent, the practice of mixing word with image is very ancient, perhaps older than that of words separate from images. Its postmedieval ancestors include the classic shape-poems by early seventeenth-century English writers, among them George Herbert, whose "Easter Wings" suggests not only birds in flight but the vessels used for the wine of the mass. Subsequent examples of this strain of worded images—where lines of type fill up the image—include the highly representational mouse's tail in the original edition of *Alice in Wonderland* and Dylan Thomas's diamonds and wings in "Vision and Prayer." Guillaume Apollinaire's "Calligrams," as he called them, take a more radical step by eschewing both the custom of solidly filling a form with words and the conventional linear syntax of all earlier poetry; the words in "Coeur et Miroir" *outline* respectively the forms of a heart and a mirror and pursue a syntactically endless circle, while the lines of words in "Le Jet d'Eau" represent a spray of spouting water.

Most of the early word-image artists were poets, but the modernist tradition also includes painters—Raoul Hausmann and Kurt Schwitters, Stuart Davis and Tristan Tzara—who incorporated words-to-be-read into their paintings and collages. Precursors of recent word-imagery also include the poet-publicist Filippo Marinetti, who not only mixed various faces and sizes of type in *Paroles en Liberté* but also fractured the horizontally linear grids that, then as now, were favored by most poets. Both these traditions, along with current word-imagery, conceptually differ from "illuminated" texts—early Bibles, William Blake, Ben Shahn, et al, and the more contemporary illuminated forms, posters and comic books—where words are physically distinct from image. (Contrast their form with Robert Indiana's *The Melville Triptych,* which is a visual rendition of phrases from the opening page of *Moby Dick*.) Word-imagery, to make another distinction, does not include the purest examples of "concrete poetry," which deal not in discernible words but in linguistic signs abstractly displayed.

In most imaged words, there are usually only a few words, as well as no image other than that made by those words, because in the word is the beginning of this art—Gay Beste's *Cross* and *Obsess*, Mary Ellen Solt's *Lilacs*, Ian Hamilton Finlay's *Acrobats*, my own *Echo* and *Degenerate*, Herb Lubalin's *Break-Up Cough*, and Robert Lax's *Quiet/Silence*, all of which are included here. As these examples suggest, a word can be pictorially enhanced as effectively by enlargement or repetition as by representational shape; and certain forms are so effective that the layout bestows an autonomous life upon the word, if not actually granting the word-image profoundly iconographic powers—Indiana's much-imitated *Love*, the logo of *The New York Times* (herein esthetically revised), and the insignia for "Coca-Cola." In this respect, the art is concerned with nonsyntactical properties peculiar to words. But what all successful word-images have in common is the sense that without a visual dimension the words convey a completely different, if not esthetically negligible, experience.

In worded images, by contrast, the shape becomes a frame into which words are poured; so that most of the time the art's meaning depends first of all upon the familiarity and suggestiveness of the shape. Among the best examples of pictures-made-by-words are the labeled wine bottles that Robert P. Brown designed entirely with uniform type laid in horizontal lines, Robert Hollander's soda container, Edwin Morgan's *Pomander*, Ferdinand Kriwet's concentric circles with overlapping words (in both German and English), and Jonathan Price's *Ice Cream Poem* which, in addition to outlining the shape and even the drip of the original, realizes a nonlinear syntax. John Cage and Calvin Sumsion's *Not Wanting To Say Anything About Marcel*, of which only a single frame is reprinted, favors a more diffuse visual space (to accord with Cage's esthetic predilections), in addition to an aleatory or "chance" bias that makes the preselected individual words less than decipherable.

Perhaps the most spectacular example in the worded-image strain is John Furnival's *Tours de Babel Changées en Ponts*, in which legible words in several languages are piled into shapes, particularly towers, over six panels—each in the original version over six feet high, with the work as a whole running over twelve feet across. From right to left, the panels seem to tell of the evolution of language; from left to right, of its decline and decay. Since the entire shape should be assimilated before innumerable details are examined, the following selection prints a two-page spread of the whole work and then seven pages of particular sections close up.

While imaged words and worded images are distinct forms, many examples of the art fall across and between. Sequence introduces another dimension, as in several pieces which have more than one image and so depend to different degrees upon the reader's turning of pages. Examples are Jean-François Bory's *Christina Story* and Tom Phillips's *A Humument*, which imposes cut-out page designs upon a genuine Victorian novel. As word-imagery assimilates poetic forms, so it also exploits novelistic ones. (The version reprinted here of Emmett Williams's *Sweethearts* was originally a page in a sequential work of that title.) Word-imagery can extend also into three-dimensions, as in Gerd Stern's *Contact Is the Only Love*, Henry H. Clyne's *Zen II*, and Robert Indiana's LOVE sculpture. Allan Kaprow's *Words* is a fourth-dimensional work, extending the art around an area and into time as well—a collaborative environment that the spectators continually create within a circumscribed space. (Kriwet's *Textroom*, illustrated from several perspectives, is also an environment, but one whose form is more fixed.)

No word-image can be understood with respect either solely to language or design; for in this medium, there is no art in or experience of one dimension, without the other. Moreover, a richly verbal field, like Furnival's masterpiece, should not, as indicated before, be read just from left to right as literature but also from right to left, top to bottom, bottom to top, and perhaps around the circumference as well; and even in the most elegantly painted example, like

Indiana's LOVE, it is a certain word, rather than another, that must be acknowledged and understood. (Many paintings-with-words not reproduced here suffer from indubitably inconsequential or arbitrary language.) One should keep in mind that this art is more constructivist than expressionist, which should explain why works are rarely signed; and they rarely reveal anything about the emotional orientation of their creators.

The visual dimension also bestows an aural rhythm—which is to say, an element of time—upon the words portrayed:

SEQUENCE

must be pronounced as well as understood differently from

SE   QUENCE

For just as all words exist in visual space, so in space exist audible words.

"Typographical devices, employed with great daring," wrote Apollinaire, "have given rise to a visual lyricism almost unknown before our time," and in the best word-imagery are both profound perceptual experiences and unprecedented forms of art-and-communication which in sum realize the classic ideal of the possible fusion, within one inclusive form, of both poetry and painting.

The following selection, most of which has not appeared in books before, intends to represent examples of the best word-imagery. To do anything less with a budding art is only to hasten its demise among both artists and audiences. (The word "concrete," for instance, has been discredited through an excess of bad art published under that name.) The major limitation imposed upon my choices, within the bounds of the art described above, is an apologetic preference for pieces in English (or the most elementary words in other languages); other constraints come with black-and-white printing and the format of bound rectangular pages.

My gratitude extends to R.B. Frank, editor and publisher of *Panache*, who asked me to compile a special issue of word-imagery and then considerately took another project instead; to Gay Beste, whose friendship and advice bestowed confidence upon my taste and position; to Harris Dienstfrey, a loyal friend and collaborator in this capricious city; to David Outerbridge, who makes book-producing an enthusiastic and magical process; and, most importantly, to the poets and artists, many of them friends, who granted me permission to reproduce their work. All the practitioners included here are living and working today.

January 1, 1970 New York, New York

CATALOG

IMAGED WORDS
&
WORDED IMAGES

in the beginning
before the alpha
bet was invented
to make words it
was impossible t
o name things si
nce they were no
t yet in existen
ce because there
were no words to
name them in the
beginning before
numbers were ass
embled one after
another from one
to infinity it w
as impossible to
count the things
that had not ye
t been named bec
ause there was n
o alphabet to ma   count the things
ke words to name   e to indeed name
things therefore   it was impossibl
it was impossibl   assembled before
e then to design   ore numbers were
ate in a convent   was invented bef
ional manner thi   ore the alphabet
ngs and events f   he beginning bef
rom A to Z or fr   n existence in t
om 0 to 10 for i   at was not yet i
n fact nothing c   what was from wh
ould be distingu   d have been from
ished from nothi   parate what coul
ng nor was it po   impossible to se
ssible to establ   ngs since it was
ish some kind of   nd counting thi
order or some so   o begin naming a
rt of series num   ds and numbers t
erical or alphab   le to invent wor
etical in the be   t exist to be ab
ginning since ob   d numbers did no
viously it was i   epts of words an
mpossible for an   matter even conc
yone to begin an   ence or for that
ywhere nor to pr   not yet in exist
oceed forward or   and numbers were
backward or in a   arly since words
ny direction tha   nything particul
t made sense whe   ssible to know a
ther or not a co   fore it was impo
herent series of   was formed there
letters words sentences or numbers

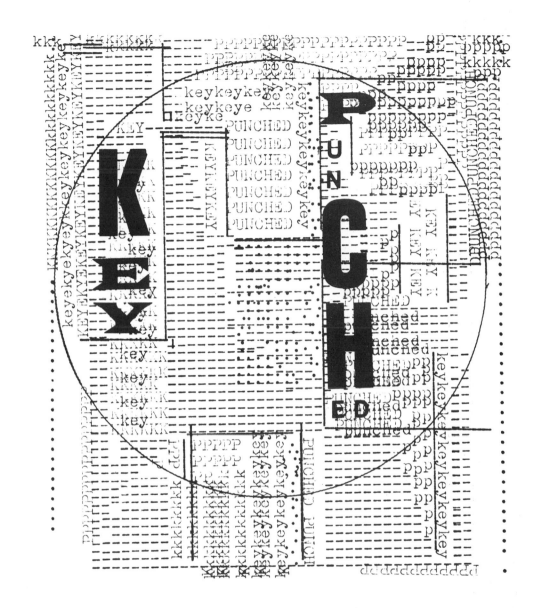

4

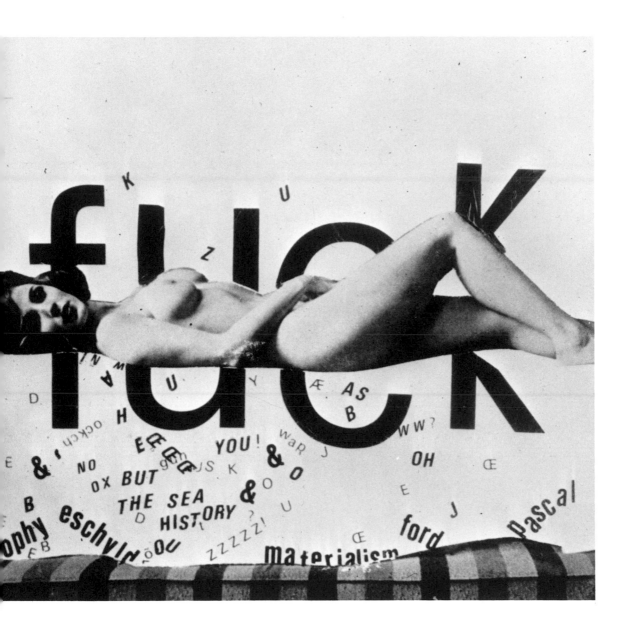

LE JOUR DE LA R...

R

RECONNAITRE AFIN SANS FIN

LAZAR,

LAZARE. —

ENFIN

POUR ENFIN AFIN RECONNAITRE TES OS TES AFIN POUR RECONNAITRE TES OS

MURMURE, — Lazare ..

Lazar

POUR RECONNAITRE TES OS TES

UN MURMURE UN MURMURE

QUE S'APPRENDS comme un murmure un MURMURE dans les les te

CE SERONS

POUR POUR RECONNAITRE

pour pour...

TÉNÈBRES

le jour, le jour le jour LE JOUR DE LA

NUIT NUIT cette NUIT SANS FIN SANS FIN
FIN FIN AFIN AFIN ENFIN
DANS DANS

DES SPORES QUI REVENT DES SPORES QUI REVENT DE CE SONT CE SONT CE FUI CE

OS TES OS LE JOUR DE LA

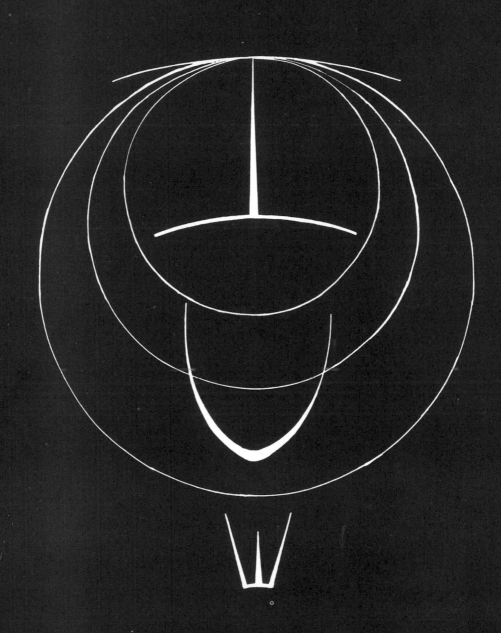

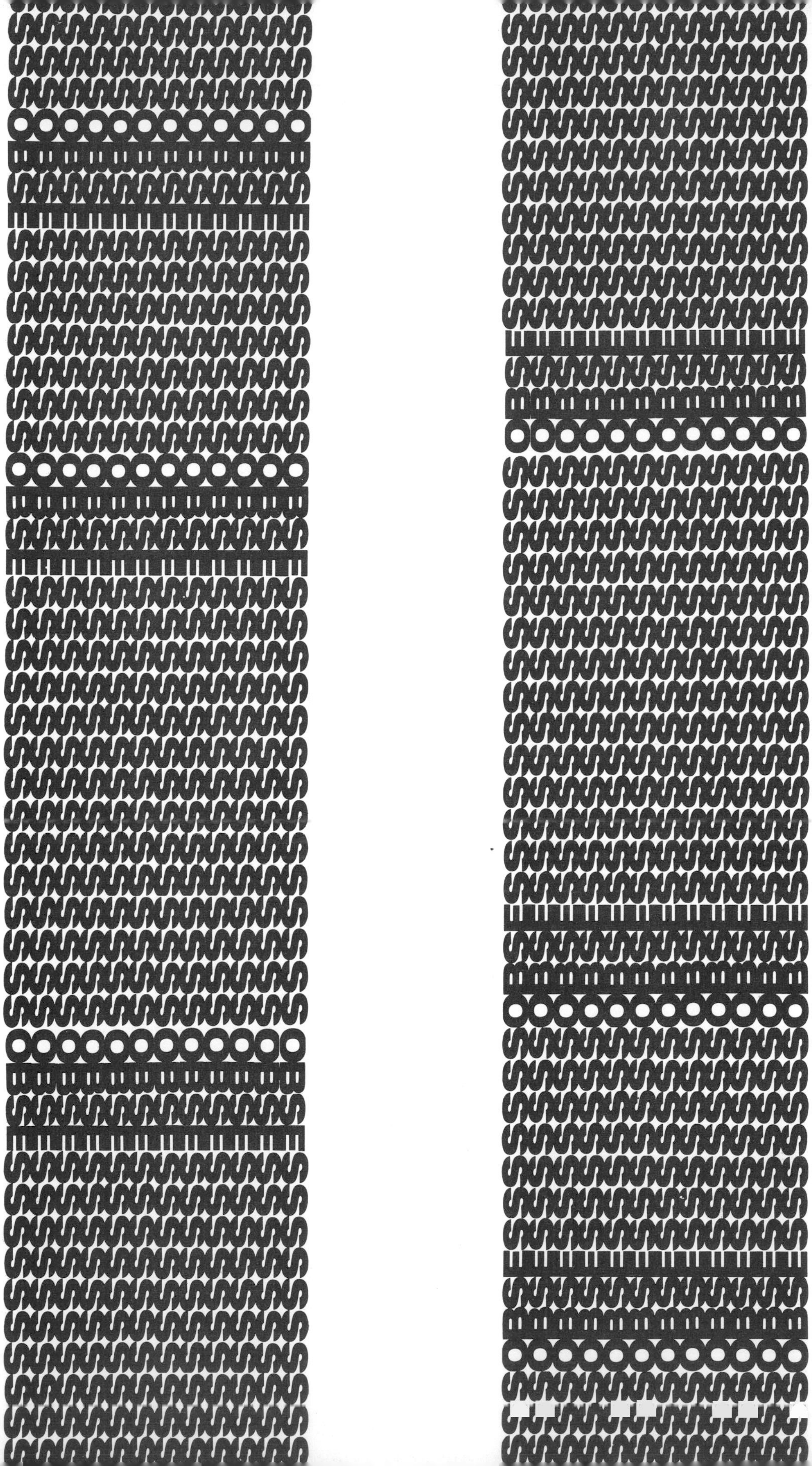

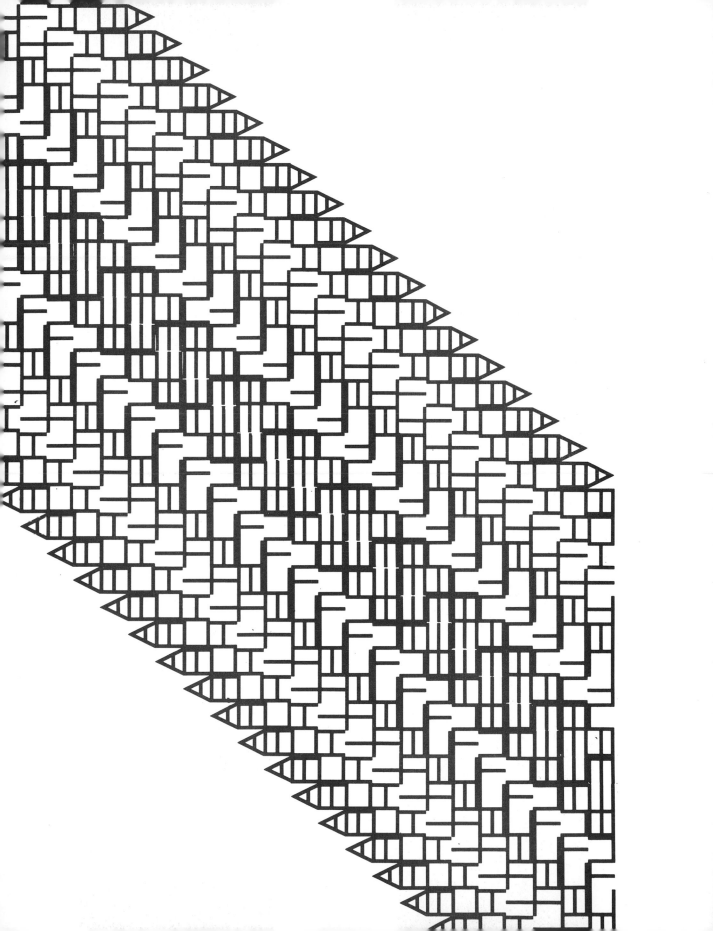

THE FIRST SHIP

to carry wine

to Britain

probably

plowed its way

across the

Channel

sometime

during the

first century

A.D., when

Roman le-

gionnaires

taught the bar-

baric natives the

delights of the grape—

an awakening which was to

change the outlook of Englishmen

forever after. By the twelfth century

there were English merchants established in

every important wine port of Europe, buying up

supplies of the vintner's precious wares in ex-

change for more mundane bounty, such as woolens

and flax. ❧ The sherry of Spain was made for the
English—literally. The dank, chill cli-
mate of the British Isles called for potent wines to
send the blood coursing quickly through
a man's veins. "Sack," long the English name for
sherry, was created for English tastes
under the prodding of tradesmen who knew well
what kinds of liquid merchandise would
bring the best price in cold, fog-bound England.
All the sherries of Spain are naturally dry—
bracingly dry, almost saline. If not fortified, they
are light wines of low alcoholic content. But
in the ninth century, the Moors in the Jerez region
invented the process of distillation, and
those ardent prohibitionists, whose religion for-
bade the drinking of wine, introduced
to the world the first grape brandy. (The Moors
also gave us, incidentally,
our word "alcohol.") Whether it was the Moors
who discovered
the magic that brandy created when blended with
sherry
in the vat, or whether it was a happy accident on
the part
of Jerez vintners themselves, no one seems to know.
The English
found the brandy-strengthened wine improved in
flavor as
well as potency during its rough churning in a
ship's hold,
and forever after sherry was a fortified wine. Then
some unsung
hero thought of blending dry sherry with sweeter
wines, to please the sweet English palate,
and a product emerged that was to change the

12

course of wine history. *Vino de saca,* the Spanish called these sweetened sherries—"wine for export"—for the Spanish continued to prefer their sherries dry as nature intended them to be...as they do to this day. The English word "sack" may have been short for *saca*—so believes Don Manuel Gonzales of the Gonzales Byass bodegas, and he has devoted a lifetime to studying the history of the grape. The modern Dry Sack sherry, which is not dry at all, but a medium-sweet wine, probably acquired its name because it was dry by comparison with other "sacks" (which at one time included sweet wines from Malaga and the Canaries as well as those from Jerez). ❧ By 1604, "Sherris sack," as Shakespeare called it, had won so many converts among British imbibers that James I was forced to issue a palace edict forbidding "the sergeant of our cellar" from drawing "more than twelve gallons of Sacke a day." ❧ Sherry could boast a proud history long before the English discovered it. The wines of Jerez were famous in Roman times—in fact, were probably developed originally by the Greeks, the greatest vintners of antiquity. Many of the steps still followed in the intricate production of sherry were known and practiced by the Greeks in the fourth and fifth centuries B.C., at the time they first established settlements in the Iberian peninsula. ❧ The Greeks often added to wines such ingredients as marble dust, salt water and potter's earth to give the wine a crisp, fresh flavor. Today in Spain all sherries receive a dose of gypsum, an operation known as "plastering." Both Greeks and Romans used a concentrated unfermented must to color and flavor wines—*defrutum,* the Romans called it. A similar syrup of unfermented must, *arrope,* is used in making the *vino de color* so essential in giving cream sherries their rich brown color and smooth sweetness. ❧ Vintage wines of fifty, sixty, even a hundred years of age were famous in antiquity, and the secret of their preservation was in the *amphorae,* pottery jugs whose surface was absolutely air-tight. Only the Greeks knew how to make such pottery, and when the art died out, about the third century A.D., wines of fine vintage could no longer be preserved for more than a few years. The wooden casks which replaced the *amphorae* were more porous, permitting oxygen and bacteria-causing microbes to seep into the wine, causing it to sour and spoil. (It is interesting to note that Louis Pasteur was searching for a way to preserve table wines from spoiling when he invented the process we call pasteurization.) Fortified wines, however, can be aged for untold years in the cask, because the brandy acts as a preservative — but centuries were to elapse between the disappearance of the airtight *amphorae* and the invention of the process of distillation by which brandy and other spirits are produced. ❧ Sherry, without brandy, was one wine that could be preserved for years in the cask because of the *flor,* the yeast blanket that forms over certain sherries as they ferment. The *flor* absorbs microbes from the air, protecting the wine beneath it. However, the *flor* also mysteriously lowers the alcoholic content of the wine, and until sherries were fortified with brandy, they were extremely light wines. ❧ Why the *flor* develops over sherry and not over other wines, no one knows. Even more strange is the fact that sherries from the same vintage, the very same grapes, will develop differently. Those sherries covered with flor are classed by the Jerezanos as *finos*; all others are called *olorosos.* ❧ Before visiting Jerez, I was under the impression that the *oloroso* sherries are naturally sweeter than the *finos.* This is not true: the *olorosos* are different in flavor, color and body—but an unblended *oloroso* direct from the vat is sharply dry. Don Jose Domecq, of the Pedro Domecq *bodegas,* gave me a bottle of a precious old *oloroso* to take back home with me; opening it at home, I was at first astonished to find it almost acrid. Yet adding just a dash of this old *oloroso* to other imported sherries made the most astonishing change: the other sherries at once became more mellow and rich without the slightest hint of sharpness. Even pouring a little of the aged *oloroso* into a glass, then throwing it out and adding another sherry creates a change, in color as well as aroma. ❧ The Greeks, too, blended wines before aging them, though the present *solera* system dates only from the eighteenth century. Huge butts of sherry are piled three tiers high under the high-vaulted roofs of *bodegas,* and each "new" wine (already aged two or three years before being graded, classified and typed) receives a measure of a "mother wine" which in turn *Cont'd on page 124*

DES ID ER ABEL

KLAN AUCHER IM KLINSCH IM TINGELTANGEL DESINATION SICKUMMER SCHER TIN
GELLT ANGEL

JEZ JERZ MICHA ERZU ENGEL

EN POLL SCHE TANZEN GRIFFEN SCHAM VERBRANNT VERWEINT ES KIN KIN AE
DOLO ERKEL GISCH ANGEL
BU BE IS AUS ALU SCHAM DYN DA MIT BATABALLBOYS PELN CHAU
TEKON GEBISSEN BOTZ TAUFNAH BUUHOMANNDIESITAELISCH TROTZ STOT BEISSEND KAU
BEL MON SINT HIN MOM NE IBLS TERREICHLICH BIEN AMO DO ZEM NE MELN
PHE ELN SYM WAS DIS JEKT O HALBE OR OB DER WRE
SYNEPHTLUTEBBEN RIG RIC WE
DER KAN DIEDEL TI SIS RE SYN IR SCHER
MAL

ZELN

18

YOU TOO? ME TOO—WHY NOT?

SODA POP

```
         I am
         look
         ing at
         the Co
         caCola
         bottle
        which is
       green wi
        th ridges
       just  like
       c    c    c
       o    o    o
       l    l    l
       u    u    u
       m    m    m
       n    n    n
       s    s    s
    and on itself it says
```

COCA-COLA
reg.u.s.pat.off.

exactly like an art pop
statue of that kind of
bottle but not so green
that the juice inside
gives other than the co
lor it has when I pour
it out in a clear glass
glass on this table top
(It's making me thirsty
all this winking and
beading of Hippocrene
please let me pause
drinking the fluid in)
ah! it is enticing how
each color is the same
brown in green bottle
brown in uplifted glass
making each utensil on
the table laid a brown
fork in a brown shade
making me long to watch
them harvesting the crop
which makes the deep-aged
rich brown wine of America
that is to say which makes
soda   pop

```
quiet   teiuq
quiet   teiuq


teiuq   quiet
teiuq   quiet


- - -


silence   ecnelis
silence   ecnelis


ecnelis   silence
ecnelis   silence


- - -


quiet   teiuq
quiet   teiuq


teiuq   quiet
teiuq   quiet


- - -
```

23

R. Jacoby '68

28

31

32

AFTER HAWTHORNE

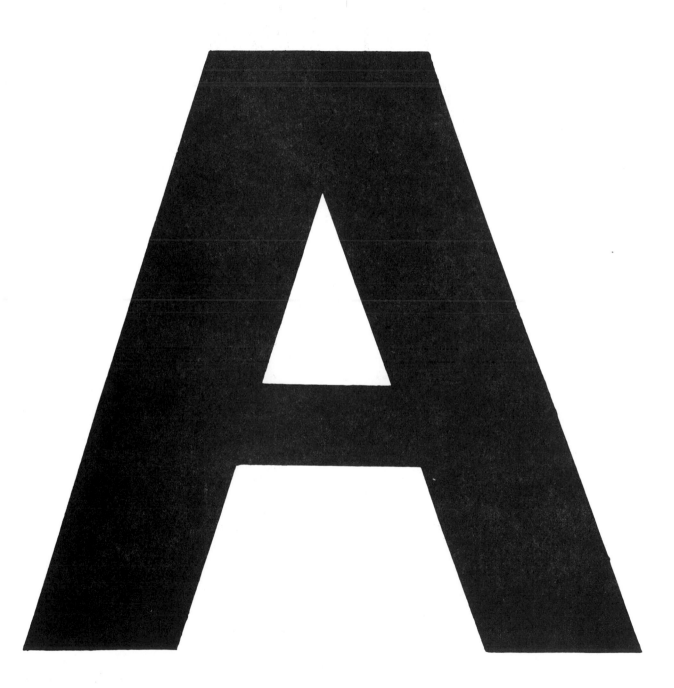

CIRCUMAMBULATE THE CITY CIRCUMAMBULATE THE CITY

CITY OF THE MANHATTOES CITY OF THE MANHATTOES

THERE IS YOUR INSULAR CITY THERE IS YOUR INSULAR

WHITEHALL

COENTIES SLIP

CORLEARS HOOK

sweethearts

s   s

w   h   t

e   t   e   r

e   a

e   t   e   r

w   h   t

s   s

Gangbang

to get her
together

40

```
                     WOMAN POEM
                       Tall
         This hair,   black   hair, This
                is       O        is
                o       you       o
                so      are       so
                         "
                       much
                       beauty
                         "
                        O

                       this

                       part

(is             wonderful              is)


           round,              round
             is       and        is
           warm,               warm,




                       white

                        Oh

                       sOFt



         and                        and

         curves      ccc            curves
                      u
         and         r              and
 o                   v                      o!
                     !



O?                                                  O



     oh-                              oh!
```

```
the    turn    of    the    screw
he    turn    of    the    screw    t
e    turn    of    the    screw    th
    turn    of    the    screw    the
turn    of    the    screw    the
urn    of    the    screw    the    s
rn    of    the    screw    the    st
n    of    the    screw    the    ste
    of    the    screw    the    stern
of    the    screw    the    stern
f    the    screw    the    stern
    the    screw    the    stern    o
the    screw    the    stern    of
he    screw    the    stern    of
e    screw    the    stern    of    t
    screw    the    stern    of    th
screw    the    stern    of    the
crew    the    stern    of    the
rew    the    stern    of    the    c
ew    the    stern    of    the    cr
w    the    stern    of    the    cre
    the    stern    of    the    crew
```

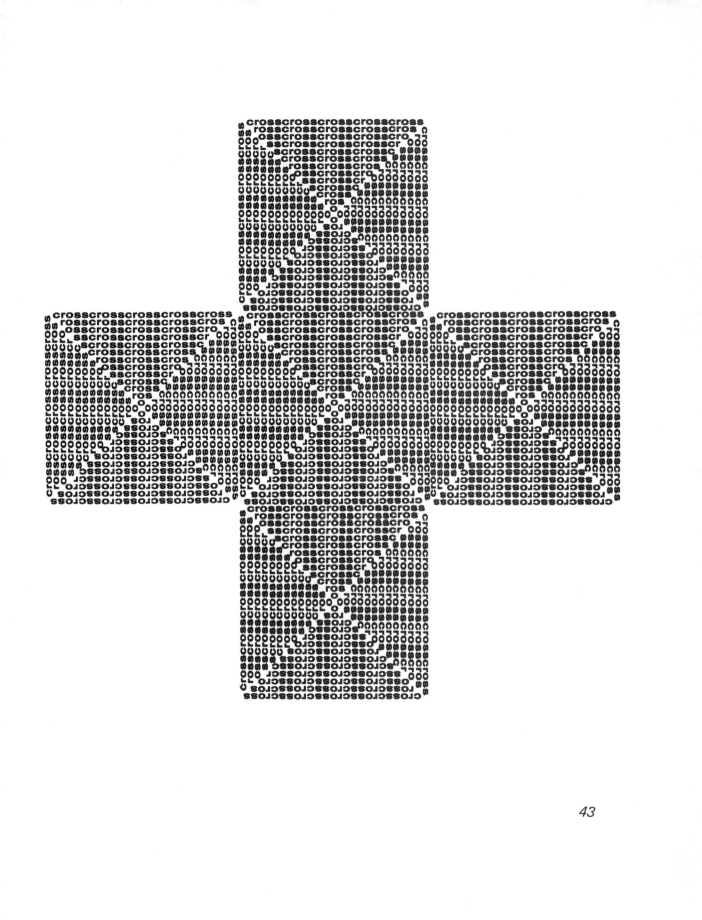

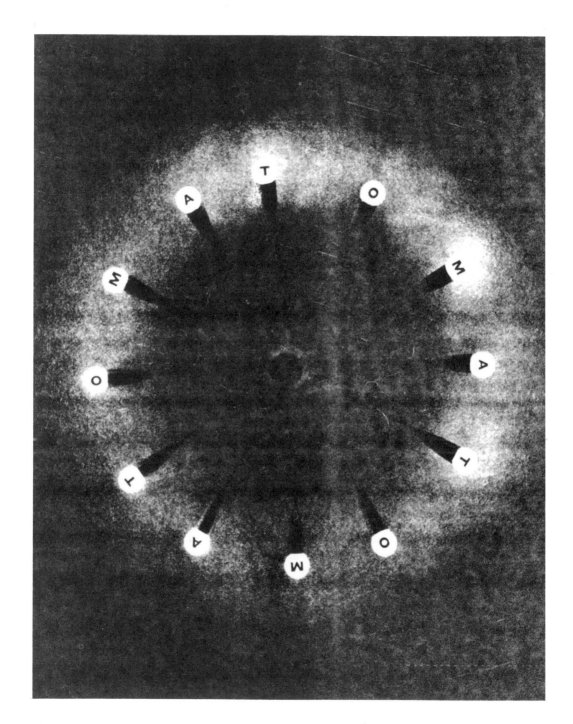

44

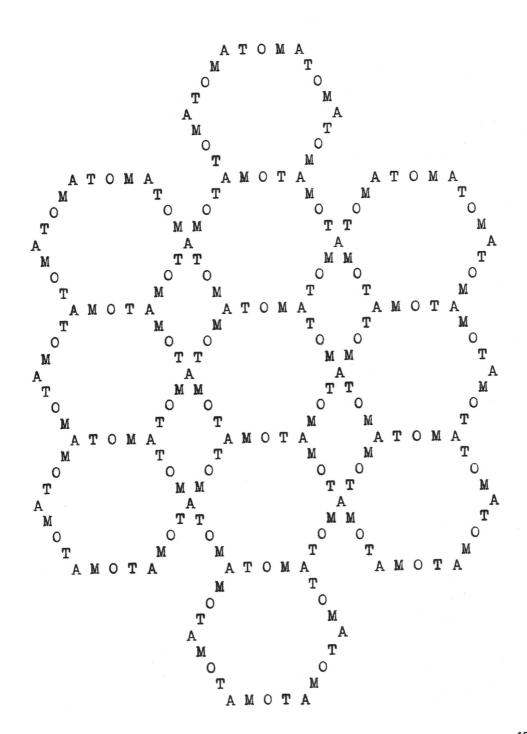

45

"rays of hope"

a
　　g

　b

l
　　　a

　e

p
　　　　m

　t

h
　　　　m

　a

a
　　　　　a

The New York Times

47

ings. nam june paik, the

korean composer who has de-

veloped ways of changing

the images on a television

screen, used some of these

ways to change the images.

there were

a number of

non-dance

activities

that I had fig-

URED OUT FOR THE DANCERS

TO DO. I POTTED A LARGE

PLANT, AND CAROLYN BROWN

POTTED IT. THE PLANT HAD

A CARTRIDGE MICROPHONE ATTACHED TO IT SO THAT ANY

QUIVER WOULD SET OFF SOUND. BARBARA LLOYD PUT A

TOWEL ON HER HEAD WHICH HAD A CONTACT MICROPHONE AT-

tached

to it,

and proceeded to stand on

her head and then was moved

gently back and forth by Gus

Solomons, while upside down.

At the end of the piece, I

rode a bicycle through the

space,

around

the

poles

and

the photo-electric cells, and then exited.

PHILHARMONIC HALL

LINCOLN CENTER FOR THE PERFORMING ARTS

New York Philharmonic

FRENCH-
AMERICAN
FESTIVAL

JULY 14—JULY 31, 1965

CAGE Variations V (Choreography by Merce Cunningham)

WORLD PREMIERE

MERCE CUNNINGHAM AND DANCE COMPANY:
Merce Cunningham, with Carolyn Brown,
Barbara Lloyd, Sandra Neels, Albert Reid,
Peter Saul, Gus Solomons Jr.

Electronic Devices: Robert A. Moog
Film: Stan VanDerBeek
Distortion of Television Images: Nam June Paik
Technical Consultant: Billy Klüver
Musicians: John Cage, Malcolm Goldstein,
Frederick Lieberman, James Tenney and David Tudor
Lighting: Beverly Emmons

THIS PERFORMANCE HAS BEEN MADE POSSIBLE BY GRANTS FROM
THE MARY SISLER FOUNDATION AND THE LANNAN FOUNDATION

The taking of photographs in this auditorium is not permitted.

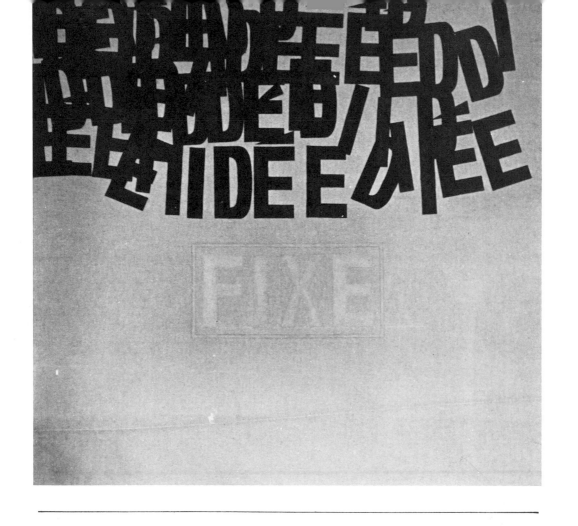

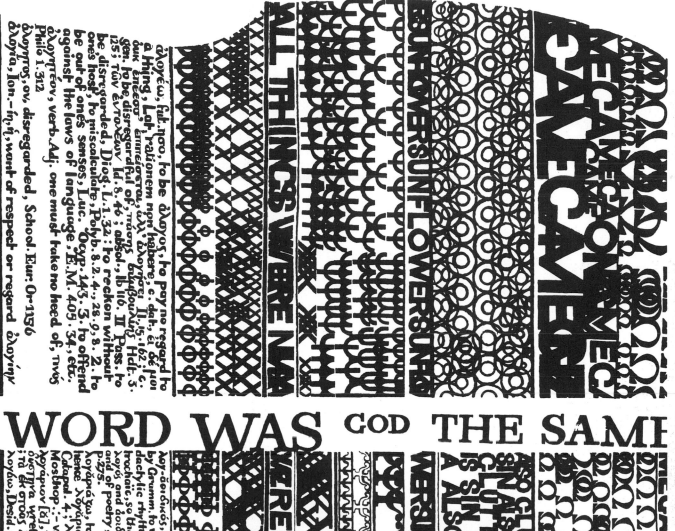

ALL THINGS WERE MA...

...E WORD WAS GOD THE SAME

WERE MADE BY HIM

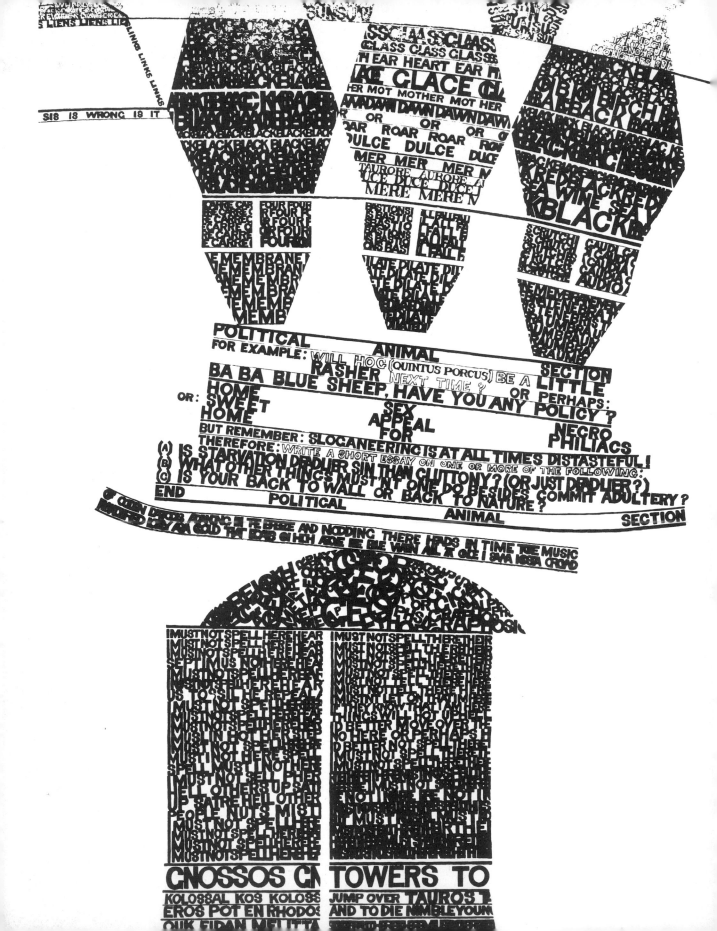

SIS IS WRONG IS IT

POLITICAL ANIMAL SECTION
FOR EXAMPLE: WILL HOG (QUINTUS PORCUS) BE A LITTLE
RASHER NEXT TIME? OR PERHAPS:
BA BA BLUE SHEEP, HAVE YOU ANY POLICY?
OR: SWEET SEX
HOME APPEAL NEGRO
HOME FOR PHILIACS
BUT REMEMBER: SLOGANEERING IS AT ALL TIMES DISTASTEFUL!
THEREFORE: WRITE A SHORT ESSAY ON ONE OR MORE OF THE FOLLOWING:
(A) IS STARVATION DEADLIER SIN THAN GLUTTONY? (OR JUST DEADLIER?)
(B) WHAT OTHER THINGS MUST NOT ONE DO BESIDES COMMIT ADULTERY?
(C) IS YOUR BACK TO WALL OR BACK TO NATURE?
END POLITICAL ANIMAL SECTION

GNOSSOS GN TOWERS TO
KOLOSSAL KOS KOLOSS JUMP OVER TAUROS
EROS POT EN RHODOS AND TO DIE NIMBLE YOUN

GREAT! FOOD! CRIME! FIFTY YEAR OLD!! WORST! CASE!! HAVE! EVER! ENCOUNTERED! SAY... NO! WONDER! THE! CHURCH...

...BEFORE! BREAKFAST!

A TEENAGE SOCIAL WORKER, MR CHARLES CAMERON, TOLD OUR REPORTER THAT THERE WAS A DOG... INCIDENCE AND INCIDENTS OF MIDDLE-AGED AND SENILE DELINQUENTS OVER THE PAST MARRY ONE? "COMMON SOLVE IT HE ADDED. HE ATTRIBUTED IT IN MAIN THE ACT CHEAP TORY JIBES. ON THE IRISH QUESTION MR WILSON SAID THAT IN ANY CASE IT DIDN'T MATTER MUCH HIBERNIA TO THIS "PRECIOUS STONE SET IN THE SILVER SEA"; IN ANY CASE, IT DIDN'T MATTER MUCH, A PRISON REBUILDING SCHEME GOT UNDER WAY. THE LIKELIHOOD OF IRISH GHETTOES FORMING IN OUR... FORM WITHIN OUR PRISONS; BUT RATHER A LOT. AND THERE COOKING TENDED TO BE... SEALED WITH... MR WILSON TOLD HIM TO "SHUT DOWN AND SIT UP" SUMMING UP FOR THE GOVERNMENT SO MANY SO-CALLED SOCIALISTS, FAR FROM RESIGNING, OVER HIS LOUSY IMMIGRATION ETC. HIS BID TO SAVE THE POUND, ADDING THAT IT ONLY WENT TO SHOW THE MOMENT THEY WERE FRIGHTENED THE TIME... PREFERRED A PARTY WHICH WAS WILLING TO ABANDON ITS FINE PRINCIPLES OF OUR GLORIOUS ETC. ETC. HE... BE TO CONSERVE THE VERY FAVOURABLY WITH THE DOWNRIGHT TREACHERY OF THOSE COMMUNIST... SUPPORTERS COMPARED VERY FAVOURABLY... AND ALL ON GROUNDS OF SO-DEVALUATION OPPOSITION, MR. MAUDLIN SAID THAT HE ALWAYS GOT CONFUSED WHEN THE TALK TURNED TO DEVALUATION GREATEST NEED, NAMELY DURING THE HUNGARIAN UPRISING; AND AT THIS, MR. WEDGEWOOD THE... ONE NEVER KNEW WHETHER ONE CAME OR POST-CO TACTICS THAT HE HAD LANDED HIM; CONEY ISLAND A DEBT OF 800 MILLIONS, AND APPLYING THE SAME OLD STOP-GO MANAGEMENT. AT A DAY AS... THE CLOCK BACK TO THE COOP OLD DAY OF SOUND TORY ETC. IT WAS THE EASIEST THING IN. MR MAUDLIN... EVERY SCHOOLBOY KNOWS THAT! BONEY TRIED THAT AND LOOK WHERE IT... WHEN WEDGEWOOD THEN... ON THE CONTRARY (SICK) IT WAS WRONG, ANYWAY? WHEN EISENSTEIN. IT WAS THE... AND WHAT WAS WRONG, ANSWERED, WITH GREAT DIGNITY, THAT, SINCE TOKTIC MARKED PLUS OTHER TIME. ON HIS OTHER HAND, WEDGEWOOD WHEN-THEN SUGGESTED THAT HE AND MR MAUDLIN'S MR. MAUDLIN, ON HIS OTHER HAND, ANSWERED, WITH GENERALLY APPLIED THE STOP-GO THEORIES... STRIP OFF MISTER WEDGEWOOD - WHEN? MR. WEDGEWOOD WITH IT A C.P.O. FORM OR TO USE A... MAUDLIN WOULD BE WELL-ADVISED TO FIDDLE WHILE REGISTER THE OBSERVER, THEN WAS DIVIDED CAIN SUFFICIENT VELOCITY TO CATCH UP WITH-SELF TO THE GOVERNMENT WAS; AS USUAL TO REGISTER THE RIGHT TIME. MR. MAUDLIN REPLIED THAT AS LONG AS IT DIDN'T NOON IN THE ENSUING SEVERAL WEEKS LATER GROUPS, THE SAYINGS OF THE WEEK COLUMN IN THE TUCK-SHOP ALL AFTERNOON ON THE DAY VARIOUS PRESSURE GROUPS HANGING ABOUT OUTSIDE IN THE TUCK-SHOP ALL THAT WAS MEANT BY HAD BEEN HIDING AND SPENDING THEIR POCKET-MONEY, IN BUT, SUMMONING UP ALL SAYING ONE, THE WAS MORTALLY WOUNDED BY HIS PEAR, MR. KERSHAW, WITH THE OTHER EXPIRES THUS SAYING ONE, THE LONG-FING, THE WORD "WAGES" FOR THE WORD "SALARY" WAS PASSED WITH A MASSIVE MAJORITY INCREASE IN POSITION. IN ITS FINAL FORM THE BILL WILL PROVIDE ESTABLISHED FOR THE ILLUSTRIOUS COURT WITHIN THE SPECIAL NORM WHICH HAD BEEN YEARING FROM THE HIGH COURT A YOUNG ANARCHIST WHO HAD BEEN YEARING RUDE THINGS AT THEM FROM THE INCH. W... YOU FOR, ANYWAY? THE POST-OFFICE IS ENOUGH. SAVE THE INCH! WHY

DON'T VOTE!! ALL POWER ETC. SAVE MAN! WHY NOT

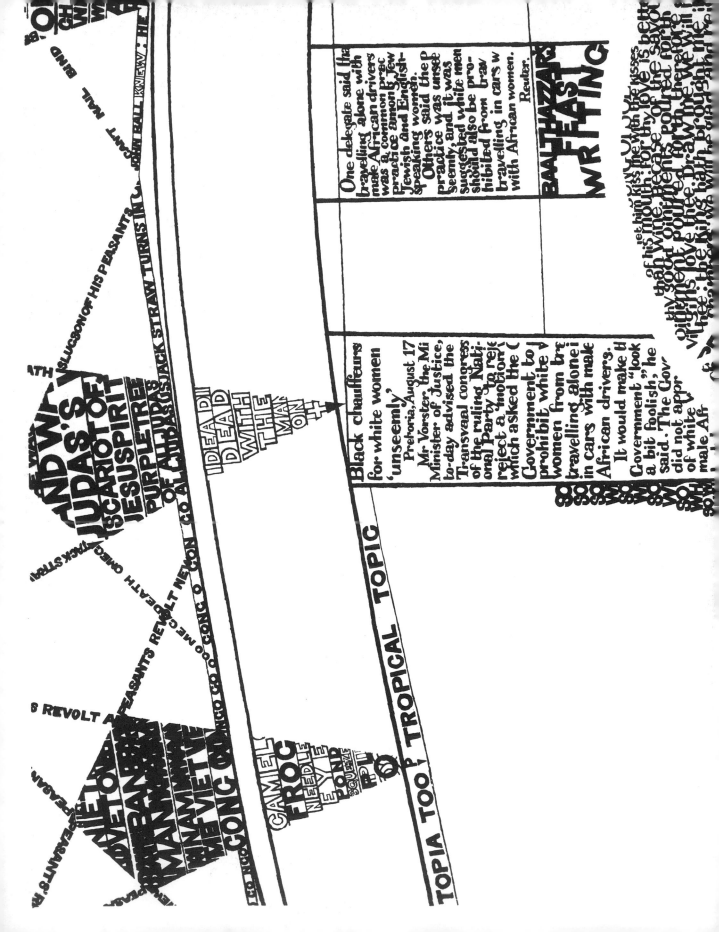

58

(MU) SE (UM)

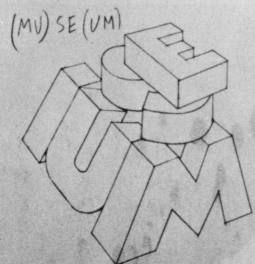

Ed

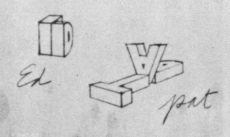

pat

93
100

Oldenburg 58

A L L O F

T H E

P O E T R Y

is illusion

illusions are a

looking of world

at the

waves of looking

finding angles of perspective points in space

and

points of view of looking as a way of knowing

looking

out and

space

of

space

points of view

                                                    r
                              o   f   d   u
                    m   u   s   n   y   s
            w   m   i   e
          e   i   w   o   p   o
           a   c   v   in v   m
              v   e   i
        s   i   s   n
        y   n   g
        n
        e
        s
        t

        h

            e

                s   s
                      i   a   s
                          of

                    tone   form
                          rw
                         o   a
                        l   v
                       c   e
            s   d
                     o   n
                          u   n   a
                                  a   n   d
              o   r   f   l
        n   o   f   o   l
      a   l   f   y   r   n
    e   t   r   o   r
  r   i   e
                             a
                             l

            y
        i t
         i   f
            o
               t   s
            i   c   p
                        e
               a   a
               n   k   61

SUPREMATIST POEM

‾ ˘ / ‾ ˘ ˘ / ‾ ̭˘ / ‾   ˄˄

‾   ˘   ˘ / ‾ ˘ ˘ / ‾ ˘ ˘ / ‾   ˄˄

‾ ˘ ˘ / ‾ ̭˘ / ‾ ˘ ̭ / ‾   ˄˄

‾ ̭˘ / ‾ ˘ ̭ / ‾ ̭˘ / ‾   ˄˄

n

n i

n i x

n i x o

n i x o n

n i x o

n i x

```
H  A  W  K
H  A  R  K
H  A  R  E
P  A  R  E
P  A  V  E
C  A  V  E
C  O  V  E
D  O  V  E
```

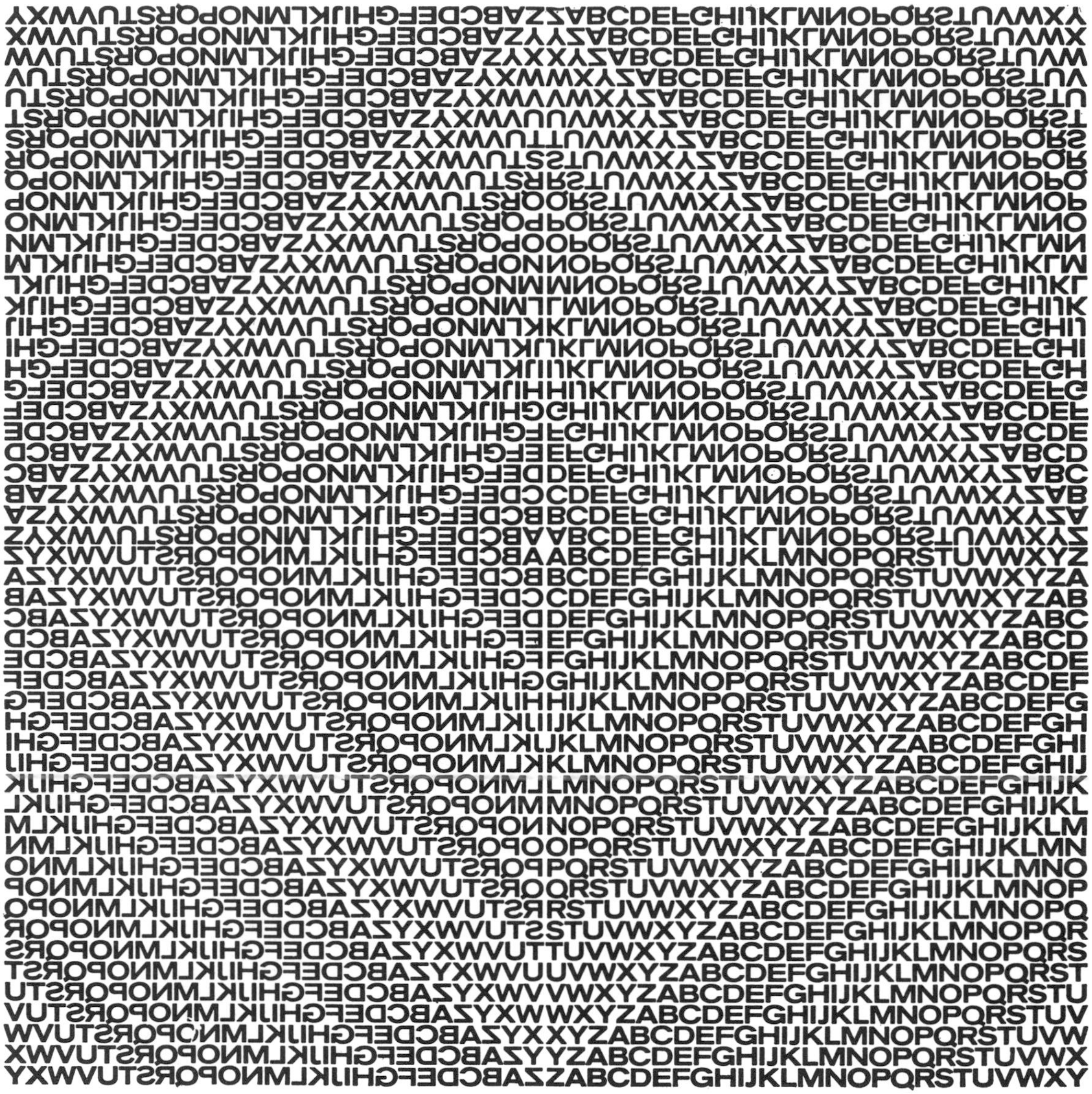

```
fffffffffffffffffffffffffffffffffffffffffffffffffffffffff
fuuuuuuuuuuuuuuuuuuuuuuuuuuuuuuuuuuuuuuuuuuuuuuuuuu
fucccccccccccccccccccccccccccccccccccccccccccccc
fuckkkkkkkkkkkkkkkkkkkkkkkkkkkkkkkkkkkkkkkkkkkkk
fuckyyyyyyyyyyyyyyyyyyyyyyyyyyyyyyyyyyyyyyyyyyyy
fuckyooooooooooooooooooooooooooooooooooooooooooo
fuckyouffffffffffffffffffffffffffffffffffffffff
fuckyoufuuuuuuuuuuuuuuuuuuuuuuuuuuuuuuuuuuuuuuuu
fuckyoufucccccccccccccccccccccccccccccccccccccc
fuckyoufuckkkkkkkkkkkkkkkkkkkkkkkkkkkkkkkkkkkkkk
fuckyoufucktttttttttttttttttttttttttttttttttttt
fuckyoufuckthhhhhhhhhhhhhhhhhhhhhhhhhhhhhhhhhhhh
fuckyoufucktheeeeeeeeeeeeeeeeeeeeeeeeeeeeeeeeeee
fuckyoufucktheeeeeeeeeeeeeeeeeeeeeeeeeeeeeeeeeee
fuckyoufucktheessssssssssssssssssssssssssssssss
fuckyoufucktheesttttttttttttttttttttttttttttttt
fuckyoufucktheestaaaaaaaaaaaaaaaaaaaaaaaaaaaaaaa
fuckyoufucktheestabbbbbbbbbbbbbbbbbbbbbbbbbbbbbb
fuckyoufucktheestablllllllllllllllllllllllllllll
fuckyoufucktheestablisssssssssssssssssssssssssss
fuckyoufucktheestablishhhhhhhhhhhhhhhhhhhhhhhhhh
fuckyoufucktheestablishmmmmmmmmmmmmmmmmmmmmmmmm
fuckyoufucktheestablishmeeeeeeeeeeeeeeeeeeeeeeee
fuckyoufucktheestablishmennnnnnnnnnnnnnnnnnnnnnn
fuckyoufucktheestablishmentttttttttttttttttttt
fuckyoufucktheestablishment...................
```

70

ice cream
i scream
ice cream

bright
chosen
lucent
sharp

blurred
rounded off
made indefinite
The side
nubbled
syrup-slow
the taste
glyceride
the memory
smirched
shimmering
insatiable

uneven
curving
but willed
jagged

the image
the transformation

eating it

silent
magical, one
ment only

melting

accumulating,
dribbling, about
the cone   to drop
cardboard
the surface
sticky as plastic

the shape itself
the texture
a test
an admission

the recognition
deceiving the mind
the lettering on the rim
arguing sugar crystals,
blatant, gummy, broken

immediate and
unknown
trivial
enormous

licked
moist
still
firm

the patchwork grill
intensifying
curving

outline
curling its
fingers
around,
and down

yet
dis-
appear-
ing

possessing

to draw, to take
in the hand,
to crunch
its one
point

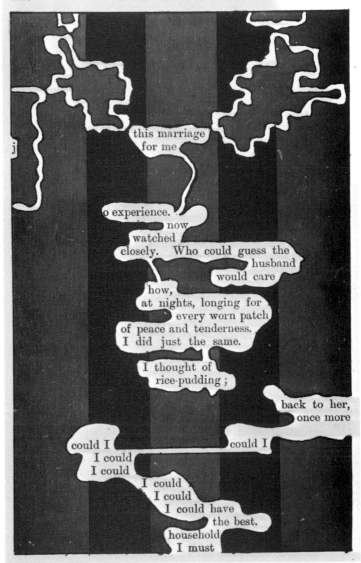

this marriage
for me

j

o experience.
now
watched
closely. Who could guess the
husband
would care
how,
at nights, longing for
every worn patch
of peace and tenderness.
I did just the same.

I thought of
rice-pudding ;

back to her,
once more

could I   could I
I could
I could

I could
I could
I could have
the best.
household
I must

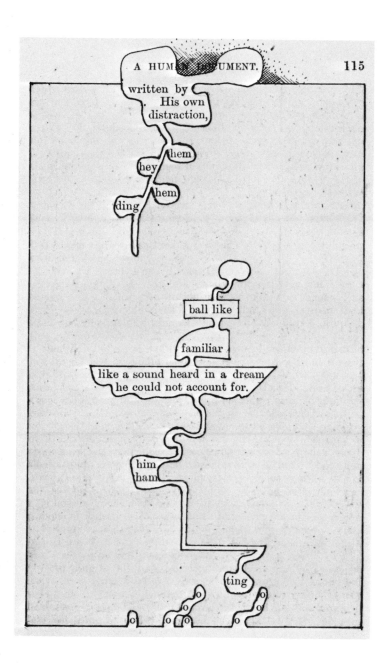

written by
His own
distraction,

hem

hey

hem

ding

ball like

familiar

like a sound heard in a dream
he could not account for.

him
ham

ting

o
o o
o o o o o

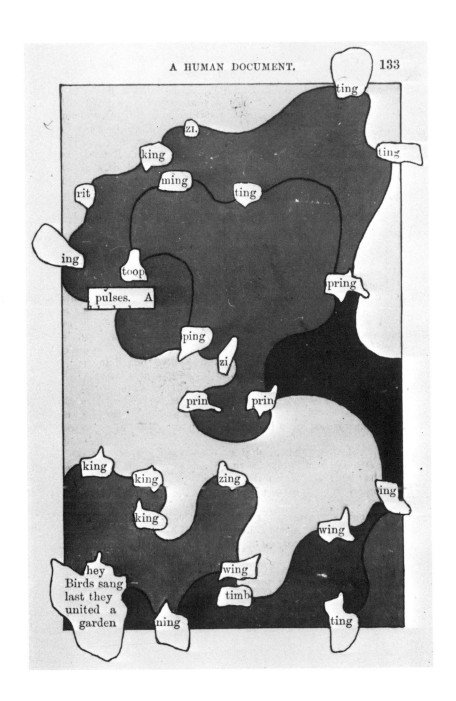

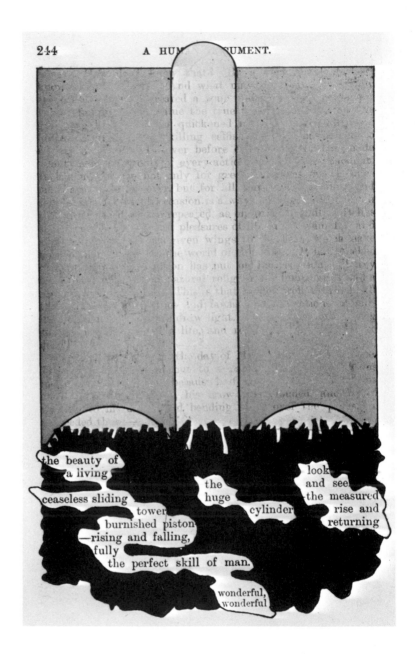

the beauty of
a living

ceaseless sliding

tower
burnished piston
—rising and falling,
fully
the perfect skill of man.

the
huge
cylinder

look
and see
the measured
rise and
returning

wonderful,
wonderful

76

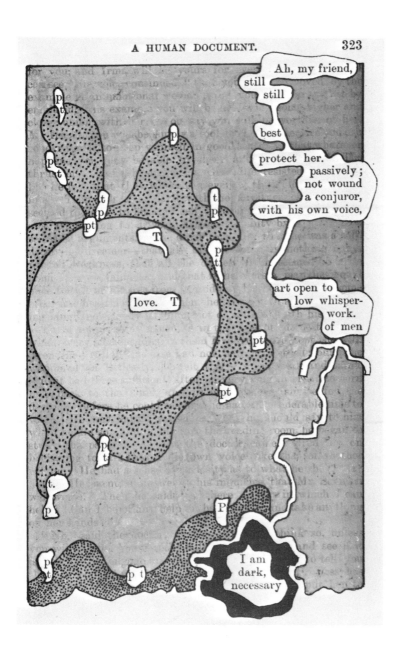

Ah, my friend,
still
still

best

protect her.
passively;
not wound
a conjuror,
with his own voice,

art open to
low whisper-
work.
of men

love.   T

I am
dark,
necessary

77

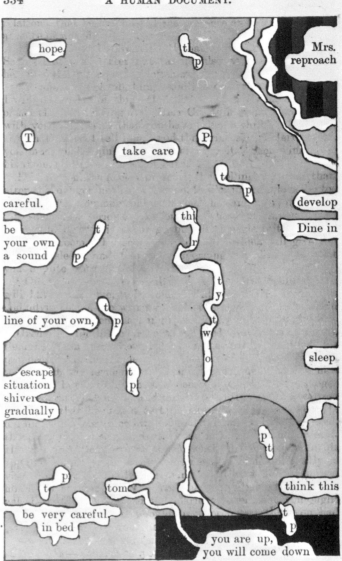

hope

ti
p

Mrs.
reproach

T

P

take care

t
p

careful.

th
r

develop

Dine in

be
your own
a sound

t

p

line of your own,

t
p

t
y

t
w

o

sleep

escape
situation
shiver
gradually

t
p

p
tt

t
p

tom

think this

be very careful.
in bed

t
p

you are up,
you will come down

```
        am              i
                              if
i am                      he
        he r          o
        h        ur  t
        the re            and
        he      re        and
        he re
    a                n   d
        th    e     r              e
i am      r                      ife
                        i  n
                s        ion and
i                        d      i e
    am    e res    ect
    am    e res    ection
                            o              f
        the                      life
                        o              f
    m    e              n
                sur e
        the              d      i e
i            s
                s      e  t      and
i am the    sur          d
    a    t    res      t

                        o            life
i am  he r                      e
i a              ct
i        r  u        n
i    m    e  e        t
i                  t              i e
i              s      t    and
i am th            o        th
i am      r              a
i am the    su        n
i am the    s        on
i am the    e    rect on        e if
i am      re          n      t
i am        s        a          fe
i am        s    e    n      t
i      he  e              d
i      t  e  s      t
i          re              a  d
    a    th  re            a  d
    a          s      t on              e
    a    t    re            a  d
    a    th  r        on              e
i          resurrect
                        a        life
i am                  i  n        life
i am        resurrection
i am the resurrection and
i am
i am the resurrection and the life
```

                    A
                   fir
                  rough
                 against
                blue snow
               or a spruce
             darkening the
              branches of
             other spruces
            behind it Pines
           on whitened hills
          above cedar juniper
         and hemlock clustered
           outside a lamplit
          window All of these
          give over hovering or
         shading after they have
        been cut stood draped and
        in a way made light of hung
        in sparks no fire burns among
          Tiers of jewels that drop
         from some eye of light make
        pools of color below Stain of
        ruby and winking mica a starred
        topaz or cold sapphires scattered
       among embracing fronds extend gifts
       Gems given in glistening shall endure
      even now the switched-on darkness later
         But eyes drop Under the asterisms
       there among the aftermath of lights
       showing up as shadow there is much to
      be given below gems and yet beyond them
       Unopened pages at the closing of the year
      wide fields with tracks across them We make
     our moments of fire last in this snows violet
    white and in finding a kind of greenness in the
    turning of white pages those ever unfallen leaves
                    Yes
                    the
                    old
                    and
                    new
                    are
              adjacent not when the
              summer burns but only
              during the long night
              From the years ground
              spring stems of light

82

                    pomander
                 open pomander
               open poem and her
               open poem and him
              open poem and hymn
            hymn and hymen leander
            high man pen meander
             o pen poem me and her
            pen me poem me and him
              om mane padme hum
            pad me home panda hand
          open up o holy panhandler
       ample panda pen or bamboo pond
      ponder a bonny poem pomander opener
      open banned peon penman hum and banter
    open hymn and pompom band and panda hamper
        o i am a pen open man or happener
          i am open manner happener
              happy are we open
                poem and a pom
               poem and a panda
               poem and aplomb

Ha not only is
   my flight true
      but my piercing strong My point is buried but not lost Asleep not
   dead it dreams
in a straw bed

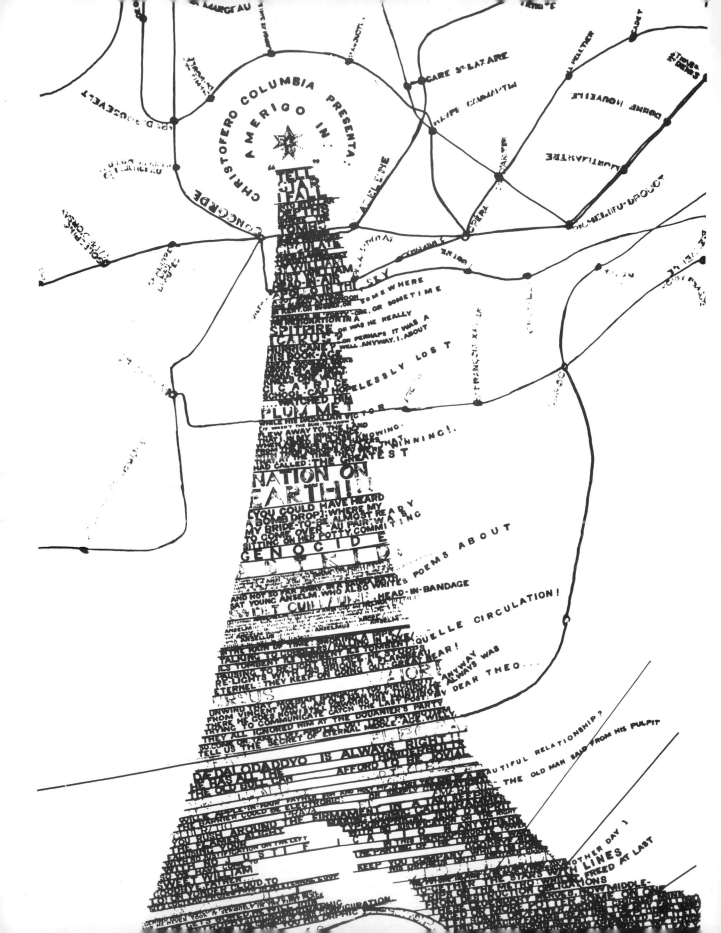

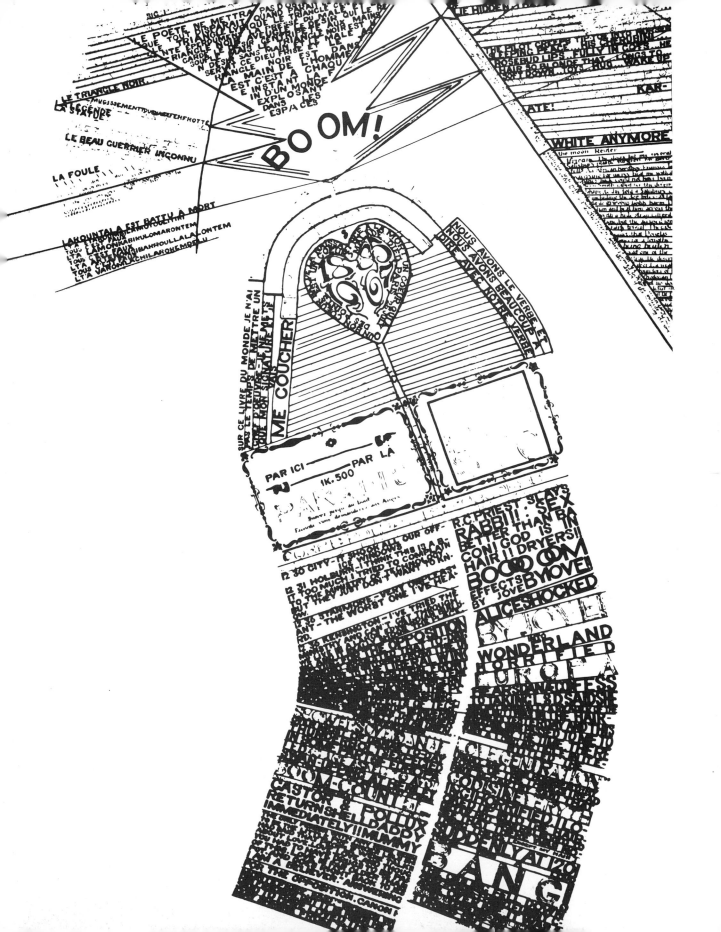

deus

snap

NONSENSEISNOSENSEINESSENCEISNESSISNONSENSEISNOSENSEINESSENCEISNONSENSEISESSENCEINESSENCEISNOSENSEININESSENCEISSENSEISESSENCEISSENSEISNONSENSEISNOSENSEININESSENCEISSENCEININESSENCEISSENSEISNONSENSEISNOSENSEINESSENCEISSENSEISNONSENSEISNOSENSEISSENSEISNONSENSEISNESS

a a a a a
c c c c
r r r r
o o o o
b b b b
a a a a
t t t t
s s s s
t t t t
a a a a
b b b b
o o o o
r r r r
c c c c
a a a a

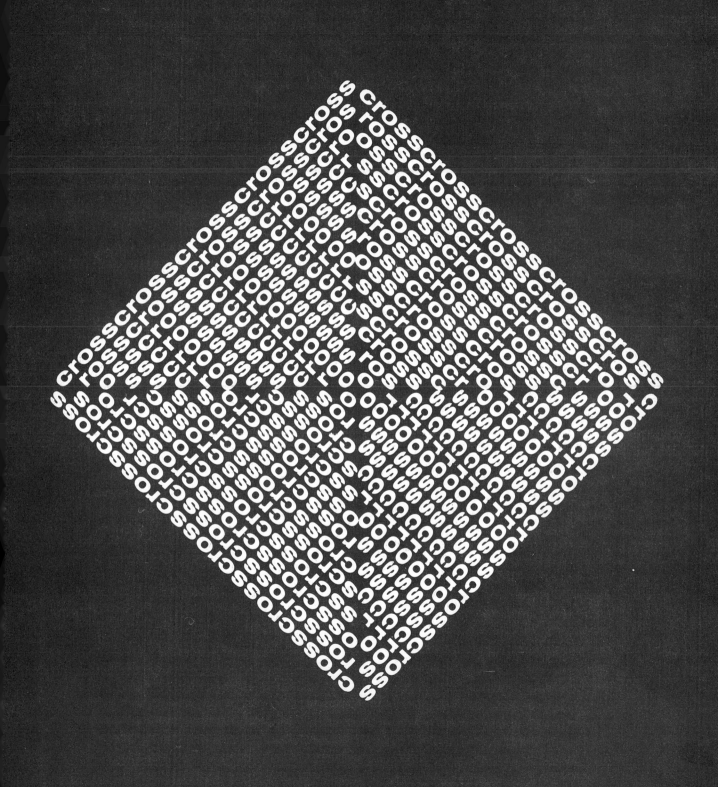

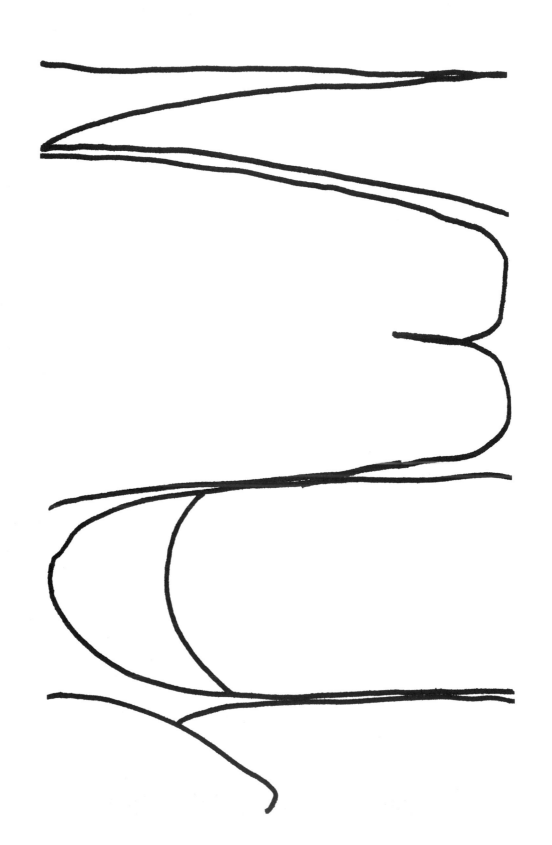

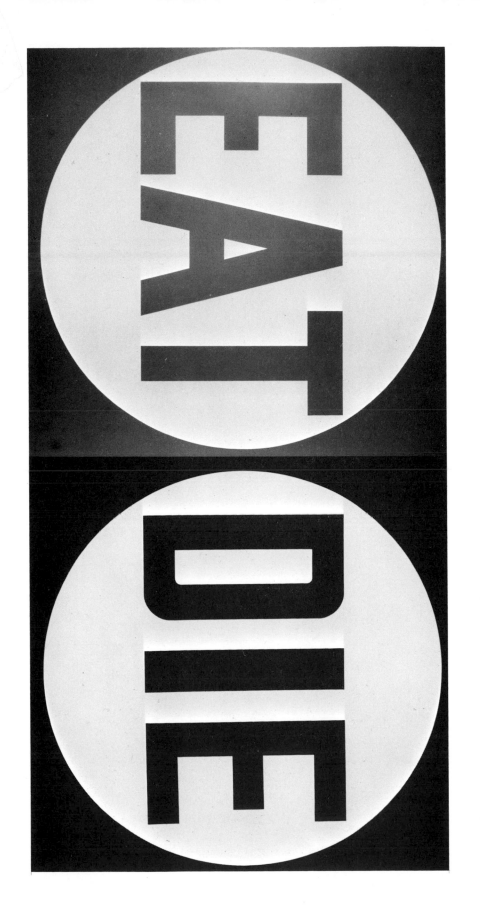

C I A   F B I   A R T
     4   3   2

M   1
O 5
M

S
U 6
N
A I 7   O ?
    R   8   9
        S E X   G O D

93

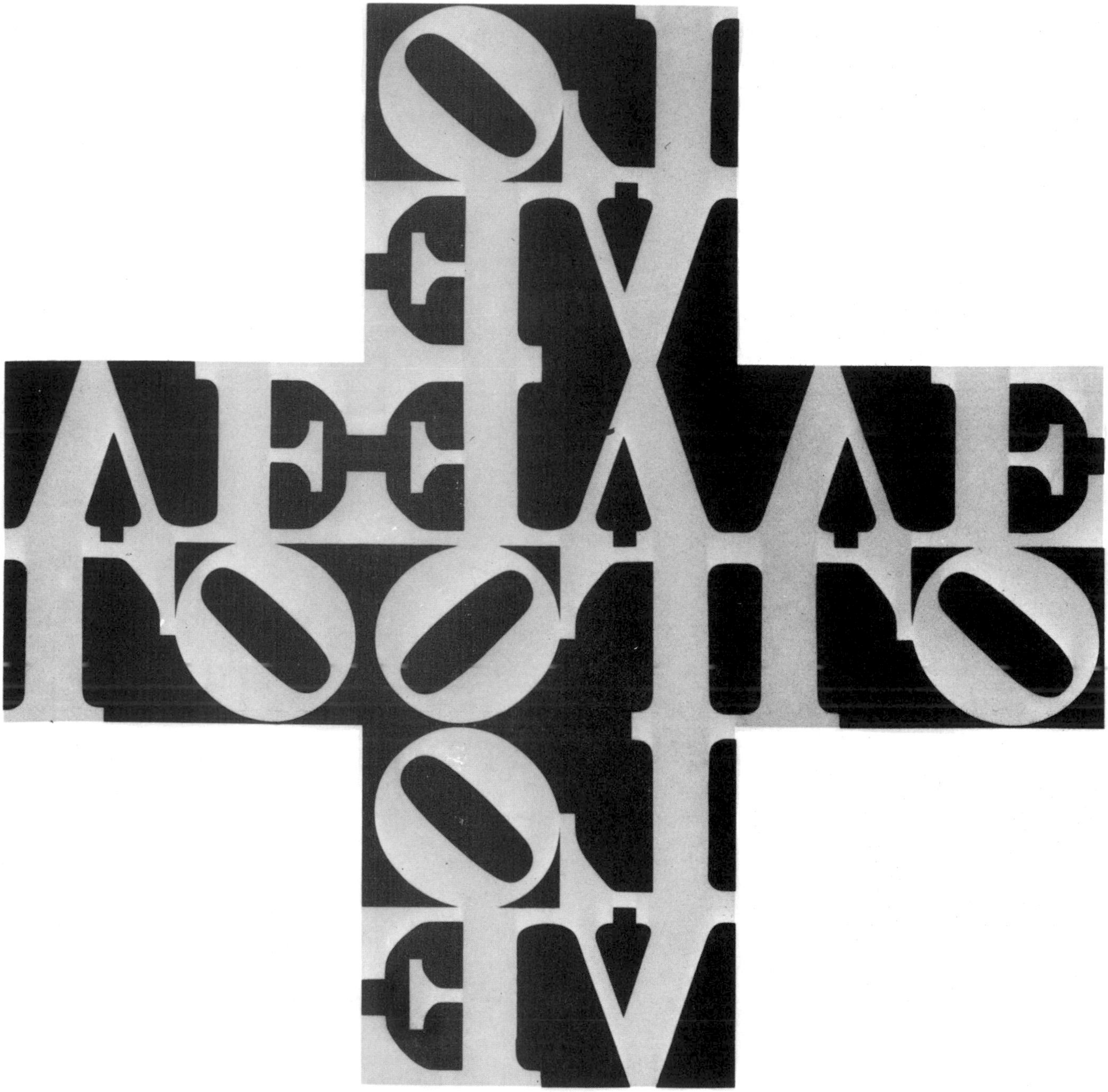

95

BIOGRAPHICAL NOTES

GAY BESTE, a graduate of the Kingston School of Art in London, was in charge of design at the Walker Art Center in Minneapolis before joining Inter/Design, Inc. in the same city. She is also a partner in Xputer, Inc., which makes films by computer.

JEAN-FRANÇOIS BORY, currently a resident of Paris, coedits the periodicals *Approaches* and *Agentzia*; and his work has been published around the world in magazines and anthologies, including *Experimental Prose* and a selection he edited, *Once Again* (New Directions, 1968). *Saga* (Approches Paperback, 1968) is an extended narrative.

PATRICK BRIDGEWATER, Lecturer in Modern German Literature at the University of Leicester (England), edited *Twentieth-Century German Verse* (Penguin, 1963). His earlier, more conventional poetry was collected into *Poems* (Fortune Press, 1964).

KLAUS BURCKHARDT lives and works in Germany, where some of his work has been published by the eminent concrete-typographer Hansjorg Mayer.

JOHN CAGE, CALVIN SUMSION collaborated on *Not Wanting To Say Anything About Marcel.* Cage, composer, poet, esthetic philosopher, has recently been working as much with words as with music. The author of *Silence* (1961) and *A Year from Monday* (Wesleyan University, 1967), both mostly prose, he recently completed *Not Wanting To Say Anything About Marcel* (1969), sixty-four pieces of words, etc., on plexiglass. Calvin Sumsion is a Communications and Design Consultant living in Phoenix, Arizona.

CHRYSSA, one of the world's most accomplished artists-in-neon, did a series of works about Times Square. Born in Greece, she lives and works in New York.

HENRY H. CLYNE, born in Caithness, Scotland, currently teaches at Cheltenham College of Art in England. His work has been included in various exhibitions.

BOB COBBING, who recently managed Better Books, Ltd., in London, has recorded numerous word-pieces on tape, in addition to collecting visual work in *Massacre of the Innocents* (1963), *26 Sound Poems* (1965), and *Extra Verse No. 17* (1966).

PATRICIA COFFIN, a senior editor at *Look* magazine, has published poems in various forms in little magazines, especially *Panache*.

REGINA COHEN works for a New York publishing house and writes poems and short stories.

WILLIAM COPLEY, a well-known New York painter, also founded The Letter Edged in Black Press, Inc.

MERCE CUNNINGHAM and FRANCES STARR collaborated on *Changes* (Something Else Press, 1969), ostensibly about Cunningham's unparalleled choreography. Miss Starr functioned as editor and designer of the book.

ROBT. DAY is a staff artist on *The New Yorker.*

DENIS DUNN is a visual poet currently traveling across the United States; his work has appeared in *Extensions*, and elsewhere.

RAYMOND FEDERMAN teaches French at State University of New York at Buffalo. He wrote *Journey to Chaos* (1965) on Samuel Beckett's early fiction, as well as an extremely inventive novel that is presently questing a publisher.

JOHN FURNIVAL, born in 1933 in London, currently teaches at the Bath Academy of Art and edits the cards published by Openings Press. In addition to a set of towers all made by ink on doors—others are *The Fall of the the Tower of Babel, La Tour Eiffel*, and *The Tower of Pisa*—he has rendered visually the works of other poets and collaborated in mechanical musical instruments.

RAOUL HAUSMANN is, of course, one of the pioneer modern artists, in word-imagery and much else. Currently he lives and works in Limoges, France.

MICHAEL HELLER, who teaches English at New York University, has published poems in *Paris Review, Caterpillar*, and other magazines, as well as the anthology *The Young American Writers* (1967).

JOHN HOLLANDER, professor of English at Hunter College (University of the City of New York), has collected his visual pieces into *Types of Shape* (Atheneum,

1969). Earlier collections of more conventional poems include *Movie-Going* (Atheneum, 1962) and *Visions from the Ramble* (Atheneum, 1965).

ROBERT HOLLANDER, who has contributed poetry to many magazines, teaches Romance Languages at Princeton University. He is no relation to John Hollander.

DOM SYLVESTER HOUEDARD, O.S.B., born in 1924 on the Isle of Guernsey, studied at Jesus College, Oxford, and in 1949 joined Prinknash Abbey in Gloucester, where he continues to live and work. His "Typescracts," as he prefers to call them, have appeared profusely in magazines and anthologies.

ROBERT INDIANA's paintings, mostly of Americanisms, have been exhibited around the world as well as included in major collections; he has also produced word-image graphics and collaborated with several poets on illuminated limited editions.

RUTH JACOBY lives and exhibits in New York City. Her work is represented in several museum collections.

ALLAN KAPROW, the originator of "Happenings," did the original version of *Words*, an environment, at the Smolin Gallery in 1962. Also associate dean at the California Institute of the Arts, he has published numerous critical articles and a book, *Assemblage, Environments & Happenings* (Abrams, 1966).

STEPHEN M. KATCHER works in advertising and, occasionally, on an extended comic work.

RICHARD KOSTELANETZ, perhaps better known as a critic and cultural historian, has also published his pattern poems and short fiction in many magazines and anthologies here and abroad—*Us, Chelsea Review, The Young American Poets, Once Again, Possibilities of Poetry*, etc. His first collection, *Visual-Language*, will appear soon.

FERDINAND KRIWET, born in 1942 in Düsseldorf, Germany, where he now lives, has published several collections of his own word-imagery, as well as created tape collages, television programs, plays for a mobile theatre, and has exhibited his work around the world. *Leserattenfaenge* (DuMont Schaumberg, 1965) includes extended close analyses of his youthful work (*Rundscheibe*); *Apollo Amerika* (Suhrkamp, 1969) is a book of "publit."

ROBERT LAX, friend and contemporary of the late Thomas Merton and Ad Reinhardt, currently lives in Kalymnos, Greece. His poems in various modes have long appeared in magazines; *Voyages* recently devoted a special issue to his work.

HERB LUBALIN, president of Lubalin, Smith, Carnase, Inc., New York, is one of America's best-known and most prolific designers, as well as art director of *Avant-Garde* and *The New Leader*, among other magazines.

EDWIN MORGAN, Lecturer in English Literature at Glasgow University, has published translations from the Italian and Anglo-Saxon, as well as several volumes of poetry both visual and conventional: *The Cape of Good Hope* (1955), *Sovpoems* (1961), *Starryveldt* (1965), *Emergent Poems* (1967), *The Second Life* (1968), *Gnomes* (1968).

bpNICHOL edits *grOnk* and other magazines in Toronto. In his mid-twenties, he has also contributed to magazines and anthologies, as well as collecting his own oral and visual work into several pamphlets and recordings.

LIAM O'GALLAGHER, known mostly as a painter, has published word-imagery in *San Francisco Earthquake* and other magazines, as well as in the anthology *Possibilities of Poetry* (1970, Richard Kostelanetz, editor). He lives in San Francisco most of the time.

CLAES OLDENBURG, one of the great contemporary artists, has also produced several books: *Injun and Other Histories* (Something Else, 1966), *Store Days* (Something Else, 1968), and *Proposals for Monuments and Buildings* (Follett, 1969).

MICHAEL JOSEPH PHILLIPS is working toward a Ph.D. in Comparative Literature at Indiana University. He recently studied and taught at Oxford.

TOM PHILLIPS, who lives in Camberwell, south London, has for several years been artistically bowdlerizing pages from a Victorian novel (*A Human Document* by W. H. Mollock); Phillips' own work-in-progress is entitled *A Humument*.

JONATHAN PRICE, currently teaching dramatic literature at New York University, has published mostly critical prose in little magazines.

ROBERT P. SMITH, formerly art director of *Gentleman's Quarterly*, is now a free-lance designer living in New York.

MARY ELLEN SOLT, recently selected and spectacularly introduced the anthology *Concrete Poetry: A World View* (Indiana University Press, 1968). Her own pioneering work was collected in *Flowers in Concrete* (1964).

GERD STERN, cofounder of the artists' collective known as USCO (Us Company), has recently been teaching at Harvard University and collaborating with Intermedia Systems, Inc. His more conventional poems were collected in *First Poems and Others (1952) and Afterimage* (1966); several other visual pieces are included in *Possibilities of Poetry*.

EMMETT WILLIAMS, the primary American spokesman for "concrete," was recently artist-in-residence at the University of Kentucky. His poems have appeared in many magazines and anthologies, including his own *An Anthology of Concrete Poetry* (Something Else, 1967). *Sweethearts* (Something Else, 1967), a page of which is reprinted here, is a book-length fiction in imaged words.

ACKNOWLEDGMENTS

GAY BESTE: "Obsess" (two versions), "Cross" (two versions), "Modular System," copyright© 1969, 1967, by Gay Beste; reprinted by permission of the author. JEAN-FRANÇOIS BORY: "Christina Story, III-V," copyright© 1969, by Jean-François Bory; reprinted by permission of the author. PATRICK BRIDGEWATER: "Tomato Atom," "Rays of Hope," "Anatomy of a Tomato," copyright © 1968, 1969, 1970, by Patrick Bridgewater; reprinted by permission of the author. KLAUS BURCKHARDT: Alphabet poem; reprinted by permission of Hansjorg Mayer. JOHN CAGE and CALVIN SUMSION: "Not Wanting To Say Anything About Marcel," published by EYE Editions, Box 30216, Cincinnati, Ohio, 1969; printed under the supervision of Hollanders Workshop, Inc. CHRYSSA: "Times Square Sky"; reprinted by permission of the Walker Art Center, Minneapolis, Minn. HENRY H. CLYNE: " Zen II"; reprinted by permission of the artist. PATRICIA COFFIN: Untitled poem, copyright © 1970, by Patricia Coffin; reprinted by permission of the author. REGINA COHEN: "History—Metaphysics"; reprinted by permission of the author. WILLIAM COPLEY: "July 5th"; reprinted by permission of the artist. MERCE CUNNINGHAM and FRANCES STARR: "Regarding *Variations V*," copyright © 1969; reprinted from *Changes* (1969) by permission of Something Else Press, Inc. ROBT. DAY: Drawing by Robt. Day; copyright © 1969, *The New Yorker;* reprinted by permission of the publisher. DENIS DUNN: Untitled poem, copyright © 1969; reprinted by permission of *Extensions* (855 West End Avenue, New York, N.Y. 10025). RAYMOND FEDERMAN: "In the Beginning (One)," copyright © 1970, by Raymond Federman; reprinted by permission of the author. JOHN FURNIVAL: "Idée Fixe," "Devil Trap," "Europa and Her Bull, II," copyright © 1964, 1966, by John Furnival; reprinted by permission of the author; "Tours de Babel Changées en Ponts," copyright 1964, by John Furnival; reprinted by permission of the author and Richard Kostelanetz. RAOUL HAUSMANN: "The Grasshopper," reprinted by permission of the artist. MICHAEL HELLER: "Suprematist Poem"; reprinted by permission of the author. JOHN HOLLANDER: "Midwinter Leaves," copyright © 1968, by John Hollander; reprinted from *Book World* (December, 1968) by permission of the author and the publisher. ROBERT HOLLANDER: "You Too? Me Too—Why Not: Soda Pop"; reprinted from *Massachusetts Review* (Summer, 1968) by permission of the author and the publisher. DOM SYLVESTER HOUEDARD, O.S.B.: "Deus-Snap"; reprinted from Opening Press Nr. by permission of the artist and the publisher. ROBERT INDIANA: "The Melville Triptych" (1961), "God is a Lily of the Valley" (1961), "Nonending Nonagon" (1962), "EAT/DIE" (1962), "The Black Yield" (1963), "USA 666" (1964-66), "LOVE" (1966), "Love Cross" (1968), copyrights © 1961, 1962, 1963, 1965, 1966, 1968, by Robert Indiana; reprinted by author's permission. All rights reserved. RUTH JACOBY: "Love," "Peace Power," and "Slow Progress," copyright © 1969, 1970, by Ruth Jacoby; reprinted by permission of the author. ALLAN KAPROW: Photographs of "Words"; reprinted by permission of the artist, Harry N. Abrams, Inc., and the Museum of Contemporary Art, Chicago. STEPHEN M. KATCHER: "Yawn," copyright © 1970, by Stephen M. Katcher; reprinted with the author's permission. RICHARD KOSTELANETZ: "Echo," "Parallel Diagonals," "Sleep," "After Hawthorne," "Orgasm," "Concentric," "Extensions," "Degenerate," "Nixon-Nix," copyright © 1969, 1970, by Richard Kostelanetz; reprinted by permission of the author. FERDINAND KRIWET: "Rundscheibe Nr. VI," photographs of "Textroom" and other pieces, copyright © 1961, 1969, by Ferdinand Kriwet; reprinted by permission of the author. ROBERT LAX: "Quiet-Silence," from *Concrete Poetry: A World View,* Mary Ellen Solt, ed. (Indiana University Press, 1969); reprinted by permission of the author. HERB LUBALIN: "Break-Up Cough"; reprinted by permission of the designer. Client: CIBA Pharmaceutical Company. Agency: Sudler & Hennessey, Inc. EDWIN MORGAN: "Pomander" & "Message Clear," copyright © 1968, by Edwin Morgan & Edinburgh University Press, reprinted from *The Second Life* (Edinburgh University Press 1968) by permission of the author. LIAM O'GALLAGHER: "Key Punch," reprinted from *San Francisco Earthquake, 3* (1968); both by permission of the artist. CLAES OLDENBURG: "Celine Backwards." "The City as Alphabet"; reprinted by permission of the artist. MICHAEL JOSEPH PHILLIPS: "Woman Poem"; reprinted from *La Table Ronde,* XI/4 (1969) by permission of the author. TOM PHILLIPS: Pages from "A Humument," copyright © 1967, 1968, 1969, 1970, by Tom Phillips; reprinted by permission of the author. JONATHAN PRICE: "Ice Cream Poem," copyright © 1968, by Jonathan Price; reprinted from *Yale Alumni Monthly* (December, 1968) by permission of the author. ROBERT P. SMITH: "Wines Without Dinner"; reprinted from *Gentleman's Quarterly* by permission of the designer. MARY ELLEN SOLT: "Lilacs," copyright © 1964, by Mary Ellen Solt, reprinted from *Flowers in Concrete* (1964) by permission of the author. GERD STERN: "Help Put the Christ Back into Crossing," "Contact Is the Only Love," reprinted by permission of the author. EMMETT WILLIAMS: "Gangbang" and "Sweethearts," reprinted by permission of the author; "Pueblo," reprinted from *Extensions,* 3 (1969) by permission of the author and the publisher. Photographs of Picadilly Circus reprinted by permission of John Hinde, Ltd; *"The New York Times,"* reprinted by permission of Anonymous.